Love,

James L. Donovan

YOU DON'T HAVE TO BE A POET TO PUT YOUR LOVE INTO WORDS

LOVE EXPRESSED IS LOVE ENHANCED

JAMES D. DONOVAN

JAMES D. DONOVAN, INC.
CREATIVE BOOKS DIVISION
BEVERLY HILLS, CALIFORNIA

Designed by Ben Lizardi
and the author.

Inspired by M².

International Standard Book No. 0-9621051-0-4.

Library of Congress Catalog Card No. 88-51257.

Published by James D. Donovan, Inc., Creative Books Division,
8693 Wilshire Blvd., Suite 207, Beverly Hills, CA 90211.

Distributed by Robert Erdmann Publishing Co.,
28441 Highridge Road, Suite 101, Rolling Hills Estates, CA 90274.

Printed by InterPacific USA / HK.

Thanks to Hallmark Cards for making its vast collection of
historic Valentines available and providing 22
of the illustrations. Special thanks to Sharron Uhler, Hallmark
curator, for the willingness and thoroughness of her help.

Illustrations from Valentines in the Hallmark Historical
Collection, from the 1800's and early 1900's: pages 16, 20, 23, 34,
40, 50, 54, 58, 60, 68, 74, 76, 77, 92, 98, 101, 102, 121, 134, 138.
Illustrations from Valentines by Hallmark: pages 38, 94.

To

with more
love than
I could ever
put into
words.

CONTENTS

FOREWORD

You don't have to look very hard at the current mortality rate for love relationships to recognize the need for a book like this. By that test, you could say that it has arrived not a moment too soon.

When I started to think about the need for this book, I thought it incredible that, out of the thousands of books on how to do things, I couldn't find one on how to express the deepest feelings that most of us ever experience.

I thought it incredible because love is what makes the world go round. And because people are so deeply interested in it. And because there is such a dire need for more of it in the world.

But most of all, it surprised me because there are so many people who feel inept and inhibited when it comes to putting their feelings into words, especially in writing.

Judging from my own experience and the size of the greeting card industry, the overwhelming majority.

Buying a complete thought in the form of a greeting card, of course, can be a matter of convenience or, in our overly busy world, of necessity. But it's always seemed to me that if people had nothing else to do, the vast majority would still rely on someone else to express their love for them.

Why? I decided I knew the answer, and that I would write a book about it.

I also decided that, for a book to be helpful to very many people, it would have to be a simple one. For the simple reason that few working adults have the time or inclination to go through 5th Grade English again.

So I tried to accomplish my purpose by keeping everything easy. Down to earth. Just enough of the stripped-down essentials to achieve my purpose.

And my purpose is *to help you express your love with all of the honesty and feeling that only you can put into it.*

—JAMES D. DONOVAN

*Love is
either
growing
or it's
dying.*

*Lack of
communication
is the number-one
cause of
breakdown in
love relationships.*

Love
expressed
is love
enhanced.

1.

Consider your purpose.

efore you start thinking about how to express anything, ask yourself: "What do I really want to accomplish with this expression of my love?"

In other words, what do you want it to do? Let's consider the possibilities.

Have you ever felt love so strongly that expressing it was as natural as breathing out after breathing in?

You didn't need a purpose, did you?

You were so preoccupied with your thoughts and feelings of love that you never let a day pass, sometimes not an hour or a minute, without expressing them in some totally honest and powerful way.

You couldn't have a thought without somehow relating it to your love. You couldn't pass a store window without seeing an expression of your love in it. Your entire being was so attuned to your feelings of love that expressing it just naturally occured. Like volcanoes erupt and dams overflow.

Most of it was probably spoken, spontaneously and straight from the heart.

What do you call that kind of love?

Ideal love?

Idealistic love?

I like *pure* love, because as I view it, that kind of love either remains pure, as it sometimes does, or it becomes diluted by the realities of human nature and the real world, as it usually does.

Although pure love isn't limited to any one stage of love, its qualities are most apparent, and probably most prevalent, in new love.

But what normally happens to new love is that it doesn't stay new very long — the intensity and preoccupation soon give way to the demands of the world in which it must live.

So instead of expressing itself with its earlier frequency and spontaneity, when no special purposes were necessary, new love soon becomes as dependent on the reminders of special occasions and occurances as old love does.

There are exceptions, of course. For just as it's possible for pure love to endure for a lifetime, it's possible for the expression of love to remain constant and spontaneous for a lifetime.

But the fact is that, in general, people express their love in response to prompting.

The prompting may be as expected as a birthday or an anniversary, or as unexpected as a change in the behavior or circumstances of the other person's life. Either way, the purposes become very specific.

Here are some of them.

Reassurance

The specific purpose may be to reinforce previously expressed feelings. Or to remove any possible doubt about your feelings. Or to make up for something you either did or didn't do. Or perhaps it's just been a long time since your last reassurance. Example:

As the years go by, my love for you grows deeper and deeper.

Acknowledgment

The purpose may be to express appreciation for a specific reason, or for that matter, a non-specific one. Or to recognize an achievement or a birthday, anniversary or other milestone, all natural opportunities for expressing your love in a relevant way. Example:

I thought I'd seen all the best you have to give, until today!

Support

You know your loved one is in need of a boost, a spiritual lift. A vote of confidence at a particularly difficult or testing time.

A bit of encouragement. Or the motivation to attain a particular goal. Your purpose is to be a good helpmate, and you know that a warm, spirited expression of your love is the most helpful thing you can give. Example:

Just give it your best, my love, and there is no way that you can lose.

Apology

Your purpose is to say "I'm sorry." Yes, love does mean having to say you're sorry. Expressing your apology in terms of your love can strengthen the sincerity of your apology; it can even strengthen your love.

Why oh why do we always hurt the one we love the most?

Renewal

Your purpose may be to overcome a breach in your relationship. To start anew. To put your love back on the solid footing it was on. (Just thinking about this, incidentally, can give you a revealing insight into the nature of your feelings, perhaps for the first time.)

You've heard that love is lovelier the second time around. Will you let me prove it to you?

CHECK YOUR PURPOSE

☐ I want her to know how much I love her.

___ I will tell her just how much.

___ I will tell her how much she means to me.

___ I will tell her what she does to me.

___ I will tell her what she does for me.

___ I will tell her how beautiful I think our relationship is.

☐ I want her to know how much I appreciate what she has done.

☐ I want to reassure her of my love.

☐ I want to honor her for what she has achieved.

☐ I want to relate my love to an occasion of importance to her, or to us.

☐ I want to support and encourage her.

☐ I want to add to her self-esteem and sense of well being.

☐ I want to help motivate her.

☐ I want to apologize and repair any damage I may have done to our relationship.

☐ I want to help regain the love we somehow lost.

☐ I want to _____

_____

_____

I tried writing "her or him" and "she or he" in every gender reference on these pages, and the result was almost impossible to read. So I decided to let the feminine represent both genders, though the accepted way has always been to use the masculine. If it can work one way, why not the other, and isn't it about time?

No matter how you go about accomplishing any of these purposes, you will soon come to that age-old question: How can I tell her how much I love her? (Or him.)

Here are some of the most time-honored answers:

1. Just tell her how much you love her.
   I love you more than anything in the world.

2. Tell him how wonderful you think he is.
   You are the best thing I've ever seen in this world.

3. Tell her how much she means to you.
   You are the most beautiful thing that ever happened to me.

4. Tell him what he does to you.
   You make my heart dance!

5. Tell her what she does for you.
   You inspire me.

6. Tell him how beautiful you think your relationship is.
   Individually, you and I may win more than we lose, but together, we're unbeatable!

Just be sure that whatever you tell her, or him, is the absolute truth.

Conclusion

Knowing your purpose helps get your thoughts started in the right direction.

What was the purpose of your most recent expression of love? Write it out in the space below or on a separate sheet of paper.

_____

_____

_____

_____

All I want you to do is to think about what you wrote, and to try to profit from it as you put your love into words from now on.

True love is like ghosts,
which everybody talks about
and few have seen.

LA ROCHEFOUCAULD

2.

Consider your motive.

In pure love, the purpose ideally defines the motive. Because in pure love, the motive behind the expression is as pure as the love itself: simple, clear-cut, straight from the heart. Pure love is never self-serving, never plays games, is never suspect, because pure love is the ultimate honesty.

Pure love is all of these things because, although it originates within one person, it is focused entirely on another. The other person's feelings and best interests are the principal or sole concern.

In a sense, you become the one you love because you think and act from the perspective of his or her self-interest as though it were your own. Because, actually, it is.

So the question of motive is really academic. In the case of pure love, that is.

Unfortunately, pure love is not the common denominator in the state of love. Even in those cases where it basically prevails, it is as subject to the compromising pressures of the real world as lesser love is, and sometimes succumbs to them.

And the question of motive, therefore, becomes a relevant one.

To distinguish between the idealistic and the realistic, think of pure love as being motivated by an uncompromised concern for the other person, and the more common form as being motivated by varying degrees of self-interest, from minor and insignificant to major and highly significant.

Having said that, I hasten to add that there is a certain amount of self-interest in everything a human being does. Even in pure love, much of what we think and do is motivated by the countless self-interests of our own happiness and the desire to perpetuate them by perpetuating our love relationship.

Seeing yourself in another person, and deriving joy from the oneness, obviously requires a healthy amount of self-esteem. And that kind of self-interest, as a base for fusion with the self-interest of another, is essential to any high order of success in love.

But when self-interest is the dominant motive, the love is of another kind.

The motives of dominant self-interest

Nobody ever admits to these because they come under such incriminating headings as ego gratification, social approval, possession, convenience and comfort, to label just a few of them.

When such motives are the driving forces in a relationship, the person driven by them uses love to serve other, higher-priority needs of the self. They do not derive from a predominant interest in, and concern for, another person. And for that reason, they do not fall within the purposes of this book.

My assumption is that you are here because your love is either pure love or close enough to it that you are predominately guided by the purity of its motives.

The motives of normal self-interest

The best of these are the motives that are essential to a high level of success in love, the ones of healthy self-esteem, as just described.

Then there are the grey area ones that practically everyone is "guilty" of from time to time. Whether they are okay or not, of concern or not, is almost entirely a matter of their degree.

Here are some examples:

You want to reassure her, or him, of your love because of something you have done, or not done. Your motive is to remove your feelings of guilt, but of course, this is a perfectly normal thing to want to do.

You express your love oh so enthusiastically, but you're really doing a softening-up job for an unusual concession that is solely for your benefit. This is one of the oldest ploys of the human animal, and shows up in the earliest stages of childhood. By that standard, it's a game that isn't all that devious, but by the standard of true love, any game is really out of bounds.

 You know that he (or she) is expecting something special from you, as at birthday or anniversary time. You could be merely complying with the expected, out of a sense of duty, because that is easier than facing the alternatives. Or, your overriding motive could be your genuine feelings of love. In other words, both could be involved; as to which is the dominant one, only you can tell.

 You are past due in expressing your love. The triggering motive could be guilt or fear, even though it may be secondary to your feelings of love. Only you, if you are honest about it, will know whether it's primary or not.

An entire book could be written about the purposes and motives of love, but I think I've made the point so that you can take it from here:

- Behind every expression of love is a purpose and a motive. And while there should be but one of each, ideally, others are often involved to a major or minor extent.

- It will help you to think about your motives, the self-interest ones as well as the pure-love ones, because the more honestly you can acknowledge them, the more effective you will be at achieving your purpose.

There can be additional advantages, beyond the expression of your love. Acknowledging a motive that you are reluctant to admit even to yourself, for example, can lead to the breaking of a very bad habit.

The importance of being totally honest in thinking about your motives should be obvious. Otherwise, there would be no point in thinking about them at all. Or for that matter, in reading this book. Pure love is the ultimate unselfishness, the ultimate honesty. Enough said.

The purpose of all this is not to suggest that you psychoanalyze yourself everytime you add a message to a greeting card. So please keep it in perspective. As something to be aware of, to help make your thoughts more honest, not to slow you down or hang you up.

Recall your most recent expression of love. Think about the motive or motives that prompted it, or that you may associate with it. Do this as honestly as you possibly can, and if you wish, write your thoughts in the following space or on a separate sheet of paper.

_____

_____

_____

Try to remember and profit from any insights that you derive from what you wrote and the thoughts that follow.

> *There is only one
> kind of love,
> but there are a thousand
> imitations.*
>
> LA ROCHEFOUCAULD
>
>

3.

Strive for the Unexpecteds.

he Expecteds are the designated days, occasions or milestones when the expression of love is traditional and hence, expected. Birthdays, anniversaries, holidays and Valentine's Day are examples.

These are beautiful and natural times to express romantic love, but they can also become so routine that they lose much of their meaning. To keep yourself in the intended spirit, try to express your love in terms of your most personal feelings and the most personal needs of your loved one.

Resist the temptation to just buy a printed sentiment and sign it. That can be the easy way out, but try to put more of yourself into it. Avoid anything that even hints of the impersonal and routine.

When you buy a greeting card, always add your own thoughts and feelings, in your own words and handwriting. Remember, your loved one is far more interested in what you have to say than the person who wrote the printed message.

Like this.   Not this.

 When you give a gift, always enclose a card or note with your sentiments expressed in your own handwriting. You can always find something appropriate to say, a relevant connection between the occasion and the

gift or your feelings. All you have to do is
give it the thought it deserves.

Whatever you do, always put something of
yourself into it. The more the better. The
effort, in and of itself, shows care, and isn't
that what this is all about?

Rings and jewels are not gifts,
but apologies for gifts.
The only gift
is a portion of thyself.
RALPH WALDO EMERSON

The Unexpecteds, the ultimate expression of thoughtful love

The Unexpecteds are the non-occasions when your expressions of love really mean the most. Those plain old ordinary, uneventful days of the week when human spirits are most in need of a lift.

Because they involve the element of surprise, the Unexpecteds have far greater impact, show far greater thought and are much more appreciated than the Expecteds.

Putting a warm and supportive note in her briefcase, for example, on the day of that big presentation shows a lot more thought (and love) than any card you could send on Valentine's Day.

As for purpose and motive, what better ones could there be than to make her feel better about herself? To help him regain his perspective, optimism, self-confidence, motivation, energy, or to reduce the strains and stresses when they're getting him down?

To do this, you will have to give your love a place in the forefront of your conscious and subconscious mind, or the opportunities will pass you by. It takes some sensitivity, alertness and imagination, but the cultivation of these abilities is worth immeasurably more than the bit of concerted effort they will require.

The Unexpecteds put the purpose of love expression on its highest plane. They demon-strate your love more powerfully than anything you can do. They are more beautiful, thoughtful and appreciated than anything you can do.

And there's never a day that doesn't present you with an abundance of opportunities. Just make the recognition of them an object of your everyday thoughts, and *act* upon the ideas that occur to you.

The great acts of love
are done by those who habitually
perform small acts of kindness.

UNKNOWN

4.

What, exactly, is the feeling that you want to express?

his is the most important question you have to answer.

More important than how to put your feelings into words, because before you can think about *how*, you have to think about *what*.

In other words, before you can express a feeling, you have to know what the feeling is.

Simple? Logical? Of course. But just enough to be forgettable.

So read this lesson until you have it memorized. Or hang it up on your wall, or whatever will help you remember it.

Let's read it again, and put a frame around it this time:

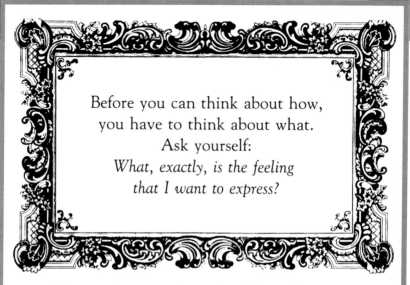

Before you can think about how,
you have to think about what.
Ask yourself:
*What, exactly, is the feeling
that I want to express?*

Now, what exactly is the feeling that you want to express?

The first thing to bear in mind is that your answer, to be helpful, has to be specific, not general. And of course, honest.

Here are some possible answers:

You always make me feel better.

You make my life complete.

I appreciate you.

Thanks for doing so many wonderful things for me.

I like doing things with you.

I really admire you.

Win or lose, you'll always be my hero.

*I can't find the words to tell you how much
I love you.*

*You are the most beautiful person I've ever
known.*

Happy birthday, my love.

Thanks for the happiest 10 years of my life.

After all these years, I'm still in love with you.

My love for you keeps on growing.

*I'm sorry, how could I hurt the one I love
more than anything?*

*Facing obstacles is always easier when
you are near.*

I miss you terribly.

The possibilities are endless, but you get the idea.

If there are a number of feelings involved, it might be helpful to write them down, in order of importance.

Don't try to express your feelings in finished or even semi-finished form. That's getting ahead of yourself. At this point, all you want to do is to identify the precise nature of the feeling, or feelings, that you want to convey. That is where you want to focus all of your thought.

It may take some time to develop a sensitivity for scanning the field of all your feelings and singling out the exact one or ones that you want to express. But this is territory that you know best; what you're trying to do can only be done by you.

What you have to learn how to do is to listen to your innermost self, and to be totally honest with what you hear.

Above all, don't be guided by the feelings of others. No matter how beautifully they may be expressed, no matter how much you may admire them.

Remember that you are you, an individual like no other; your loved one and the life you share is like no other. It certainly follows that your feelings are unique to you, and to the two of you.

What you want to isolate is the particular feeling that you want to express at this particular time.

When you think you have it, ask yourself if it's as specific as it ought to be. The more you can pinpoint the *exact* feeling you want to express, the better you will be able to express it.

*Love lieth deep;
love dwells not
in lip-depth.*

ALFRED TENNYSON

5.

Now that you know the feeling you want to express, what should you do with it?

he first thing you should do is to say it out loud or write it down. Because the most direct, and often most effective, way to express a feeling is to express it just the way it came to you.

For example, if the thought that came to you was, *"You make me feel good,"* you could express it exactly that way, just as you felt it. *"You make me feel good"* is simple, honest, sincere, right out of your innermost self, completely unfettered, unfussed with. It has a sense of spontaneity, power and truth that you'd probably find difficult to improve upon.

The reason is that the shortest distance

between two points is always a straight line. So the best advice is *to say it like you feel it.*

Don't try to be clever. And don't try to be anyone other than yourself. Remember, *you* are the one he or she wants to hear it from, straight from *your* heart, in *your* words. Because the tightest human connection also happens to be a straight line, between two hearts.

If you can convey the pure honesty of your feelings, you'll never have to worry about being an effective communicator. You do not have to be born with a gift for words to get your feelings across.

Isn't that all you're trying to do, to get your true feelings across?

Another example:

Say the feeling you want to express is: *"I like being with you."*

What's wrong with expressing it just that way?

Usually, your feeling will take some thought, and probably some trial and error, to end up with something that really says it for you, in a way that you will feel right about. But in the case of this example, you really wouldn't have to change a word.

Can you think of a way to say it that would be more to the point, that would be more sincere, that would make him or her feel better?

If you think that you can, then you absolutely have to try. But before you do, it would be a good idea to examine the feeling itself and the simple, honest thought that came along with it.

One more:

Let's say the feeling you want to express is *"I like doing things with you."* You could work on that for a long time, or you could say it just the way you thought about it. It's simple, straight to the point, sincere, and seems to say it all for you.

But you might have some specific examples that you want to add that would make the message even more meaningful. Good, you should do that.

Trust your instincts, because only you know your feelings and the nuances of your totally unique relationship.

It all depends, too, on the context. Is it a short message written on a greeting card, or is it a note, or a letter? The scope of what you say will be affected accordingly.

Again, trust your instincts, and if in doubt, be guided by the test of common sense.

You are my best friend.

You are the best thing that ever happened to me.

Thanks for marrying me.

All of these could be basic feelings for expression. And they appear hard to improve upon. So if it meets that kind of test, consider going with what you've got, at least as a starting point.

The words that come to you along with your feelings are often meaningful because they are not accidental or coincidental. And the reason they are not is that the subconscious self, sometimes called the intuitive self, is often quicker and wiser than the conscious one.

Let's assume now that you know the feeling you want to express, but you aren't getting any inspiration from the feeling itself.

You don't know where to start, because you fear that anything you say is going to be an embarassment, because you have little or no confidence in your ability to express yourself.

Especially in writing.

What you really want to know is:

How do you come up with words that will say what you want to say, and that you can be proud of?

The first answer is, easier than you think.

Like anything that you are convinced you can't do, the first thing you should do is to stop saying you can't do it. Could a baseball player ever get a hit if he were convinced he couldn't?

Millions of people are "no good" at math, or at understanding music, simply because they were never taught how to understand the subject in the beginning, to see the fascinating, satisfying side of it rather than the difficult, fearsome thing that their teachers made it. But for the rest of their lives, these people are convinced that the reason is their inborn lack of ability.

Most people lack confidence in their ability to put their feelings into words for the same reason.

So from this moment on, never again say, either out loud or to yourself, that you are no good at expressing yourself. If you can do that, you'll be five miles down the road before you begin.

The fact of the matter is, if you can feel love, you can express love. All you really have to do is to let down the barriers of your inhibitions and let the feelings come out, just as you feel them.

The other thing you should do is to stop thinking of what you can't do as one big impossible problem, because when you break it down, all that's really involved is a number of simple steps that are very easy to learn.

And the first one is the simplest.

6.

Make it simple.

It's likely that much of the love expression you most admire and respect as a standard to be emulated is far from simple.

Consider how we've been conditioned by Shakespeare and all the other classic writers whose long, flowery words and phrases are such a memorable part of our favorite love poems, stories and movies.

Yes, they moved us to unforgettable emotion, and sometimes tears. So naturally, our present standards of great love expression have been largely influenced by those memories, especially the ones of our most impressionable years.

You don't have to change a thing about those cherished memories; I wouldn't think of asking that. But I am going to ask that you adopt a new standard of expression and communication:

Simple is better.

Simply because simple communicates better. It says what you want to say more directly, clearly, honestly, sincerely, powerfully and memorably. With all due respect for the classics, aren't these the very reasons that motivate you to express your love in the first place?

Here are two facts of communication that you should commit to memory:

1. *Short, easy words are better than long, hard ones.*
2. *Short, simple sentences are better than complicated ones.*

You'll find, as most experienced writers have, that your best sentences are the short, uncluttered, straight-ahead ones that your English teacher called declarative. Sentences consisting of a subject, verb and object, in that order. Like *"I love you."*

Simple sentences are not only easier to understand, they are also easier to write. They also help keep your thoughts clear and on the track.

Avoid complex, involved sentences with too many clauses and modifying phrases. The best way to do that is to simply not write sentences with a lot of words.

If you write something that's overly long and complicated, just break it down into shorter sentences, without worrying too much about the rules of sentence structure and punctuation. Just read it back to yourself against these two simple tests:

☐ Does it say what you want it to say?
☐ Will it be clear to the one you are writing it to?

If you can satisfy yourself on these two counts, give yourself an "A" and wrap it up.

Consider the following examples:

I love you because I admire and trust you and like being with you because you make me feel good, and you've got the cutest little nose I ever tweaked, and oh, there are more reasons than I can count!

The above sentence may succeed in getting its point across, but notice how much sharper each thought becomes when the sentence is broken down into a number of short ones:

I love you for more reasons than I can count. I admire you. I trust you. I like being with you. You make me feel good. And you've got the cutest little nose I ever tweaked!

Whenever you write a sentence that seems too long, try breaking it down into shorter sentences, as in the above example where each separate thought became a sentence of its own.

Use commas at those places where you feel the need for a pause, not necessarily where your English teachers told you to use them, and use periods at those places where you feel the need for a stop. *You* be the judge, using no other test than the one of comprehension:

Will the particular meaning you want to convey be clearly understood by the person you are directing it to? If you feel that it will, go with what you have written.

This not to suggest, however, that you never write anything but short, simple, declarative sentences (like "I love you"). If you're writing a message of some length, a letter for example, that would soon get monotonous.

So try for some variety and change of pace. Here, for example, are three sentences of moderate length followed by one short one:

I looked for her every time I turned a corner.
I felt my hopes go up every time a door opened.
I searched without knowing what she looked like.
Then I saw you!

The first three sentences create a pattern that, after the first two, creates a sense of predictability, which the third repetition verifies. The fourth sentence comes as a surprise, and demonstrates how change of pace can add interest to whatever you write.

But don't worry about phrasing and sentence structure too much. Write what you want to say as clearly and as expressively as you can; try saying it as many different ways as you have the time and patience to try.

But don't make the mistake of becoming too preoccupied with technique. *What* you say and the honesty with which you say it is far more important, so that is where you should put the greatest amount of your time and effort.

When it comes to form versus content, content almost always wins. In the art of love expression, it always does.

The use of adjectives

Adjectives are the words (like *pretty*) that describe nouns (like *picture*) and pronouns (like *girl*). They are obviously used a lot in love to describe the attributes of a loved one.

If there is any form of communication in which an unlimited use of adjectives would seem to be justified, it would have to be in the expression of love.

It is also true that, as an enthusiastic lover, you are licensed to overrule any law of grammar that prevents you from expressing your feelings exactly as you feel them.

Nevertheless, I encourage you to consider the merits of understatement, not necessarily as a policy to be rigidly enforced but as something to think about and possibly experiment with as you progress.

Consider, for example, the following two sentences:

You are the greatest, most beautiful, wonderful, fantastic person I have ever known.

Here is the same thought with the adjectives reduced to one:

You are the most beautiful person I have ever known.

Which, in your opinion, is the more powerful? The more sincere? The more convincing?

My advice is to use adjectives as the descriptive tools that they are, in whatever number you feel best describes your thoughts and feelings. A long series of them, for example, extolling the honestly felt attributes of a loved one, can convey a tremendous amount of exuberence and conviction. And that's priceless.

But every now and then, just for variety, give understatement and simplicity a chance. They will rarely let you down.

Here are some more ways to achieve simplicity:

Don't try to express too many different feelings in one communication. Try to stay with the feeling you started out with; one is usually preferable, unless there is a highly related connection with others. You can usually get other important thoughts or feelings across more effectively if you express them separately, so that you can give them all the importance they deserve.

Don't confuse simplicity with brevity, although there is nothing wrong with brevity as long as it doesn't short-change your purpose. You don't want to talk or write like a telegram, because extreme brevity, especially if it lacks an offsetting warmth, may be perceived as abrupt, hurried and short on care, qualities that are hardly conducive to the purpose of a love message.

There is an infinite number of ways to say I love you, but it's interesting to note that the most often-used expression in the history of romantic love consists of those three little words, "I love you." The world has been trying to improve upon them for centuries, but it appears that even the greatest poets and writers have not been able to do so. This is perhaps the most convincing argument for simplicity. My point is this. Express your love as many different ways as you can, but don't overlook the power of the ultimate simplicity, "I love you."

When you've said what you want to say, stop. How long should it be? As long as it takes to say what you want to say. You'll have to use your judgment on that, because it's something that only you will know. Trust yourself.

EXAMPLES OF SIMPLICITY

I love you.

I like you.

You make me feel good.

Wherever you go, my heart goes with you.

Every day I love you more.

How did you ever get so wonderful?

Thanks for marrying me.

You are the No.1 person in my life.

There is nothing I wouldn't do for you.

Everything beautiful reminds me of you.

I like being with you.

I like the way you look.

I like the way you talk.

I like the way you think.

I like everything about you.

I like you just the way you are.

You are incredible!

You are the best thing I've ever seen in this world.

You are my hero.

You are the one.

Your eyes tell me everything about you.

Your voice is my favorite music.

I like it when you do that.

I miss you.

I wish you were here with me.

Love me or leave me.

I like to walk with you.

I like to talk with you.

I like to do everything with you.

Will you marry me?

I will.

Less is more.

ROBERT BROWNING

7.

Make it sincere.

f all the qualities that make for success in the expression of love, sincerity is by far the most important.

You can put all of the other qualities into what you say or write, but if it hasn't got sincerity, it will not serve your purpose, and may even work against it.

How do you achieve sincerity? And how do you avoid insincerity?

Mostly by being true to yourself.

By never doing anything that is out of character for you, that isn't the real you.

By never doing anything for superficial effect.

By never doing anything that is against your

best judgment, or your instincts.

By employing your own honest style, limitations and all, rather than trying to emulate what you may think is the superior style of someone else.

Your No.1 rule should be to let honesty be your guide. In everything you do, say or write. There are other considerations, of course, but the most critical one is your own sense of truth.

Here is an example of how honesty can help you distinguish between sincerity and in-sincerity.

It concerns flattery, which is nice to give and as nice or nicer to receive. We all have egos and a perpetual need for shoring them up.

But beware! There is a line you must never cross, and that is the line of insincerity. Cross it by a hair, and the person on the other side will know it in an instant.

In many ways, the one who loves you knows you better than you know yourself. So while you may misjudge the line between sincerity and insincerity, he or she never will.

If in doubt, ask yourself:

Is this how I really feel? I mean _really_?

Am I exaggerating the truth just a bit too much here?

Does it sound sincere to me?

Does it sound like me?

Is it in the best of taste; could it be misinterpreted?

Is it respectful of his or her needs, ego and self-interest, as opposed to my own?

Am I using flattery just to serve my personal advantage, as the easiest way home? Or is this honestly what I feel and want to express for that reason alone?

Sincerity can be achieved with virtually any style that is natural to you. But it may be helpful to remember that a touch of unselfish (even self-effacing) humility tends to enhance the degree of sincerity. To the extent, of course, that it is honest.

To repeat. The most helpful and reliable test of sincerity is your own sense of honesty. If it isn't totally honest, forget it.

> *The heart is a brittle thing,*
> *and one false vow can break it.*
>
> E.G. BULVER-LYTTON
>
>

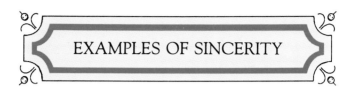

EXAMPLES OF SINCERITY

Thank you.

I'm sorry.

I was wrong.

Please forgive me.

You are right.

Let's do it your way.

OK, now tell me how you feel about it.

You bring out the best in me.

I like doing things with you.

I like doing things for you.

You are the best thing that ever happened to me.

You are my best friend.

Thank you for all the happiness you have given me.

I like you.

I like you as much as I love you.

I feel complete when you hold my hand.

As beautiful as you are on the outside, you are even more beautiful on the inside.

You are the greatest gift of my life.

I used to think about my best interests. Now I think about ours, and yours more than mine.

Thank you for giving me everything I ever wanted.

Thank you for teaching me how to fly.

You are my greatest source of excitement, and peace.

When I found you, I found myself.

I never thought I had a chance with you.

You inspire me, because you are everything I respect and admire.

I don't think I ever trusted anyone a hundred percent, until the moment I looked into your eyes.

Just being with you is the nicest thing that ever happened to me.

I feel proud just to walk down the street with you.

8.

Make it reek with feeling!

Warmth.
Tenderness.
Care.
Empathy.
Excitement.
Passion.
Contentment.
Whatever you feel.

eelings are highly contagious. And when expressed with spontaneity, sincerity and intensity, they can be literally transmitted from one person to another, either as spoken words or right off the paper they're written on!

Ask yourself. What is love without feeling? What is love without warmth, and tenderness, and caring, and excitement, and passion? What is love if not alive with all of these feelings?

My advice is to never be afraid to let your emotions show. It's true that we all have our

own style, and that we should not try to conform to behavior that is unnatural or next to
impossible for us. Granted.

I am not suggesting that introverts express
themselves like flamboyant extroverts. I am
suggesting that, no matter what your personality type or style, you should be able to find a
natural way to let your emotions show, with
genuine feeling.

If love is an emotional experience, doesn't it
simply follow that we will be more successful in
expressing our love if we allow the full force of
our emotions to show, so that the other person
can feel the intensity?

Whatever your personality type, I hope you
will see the simple logic of that question and go
along with this suggestion:

Whatever your emotion, let it show. In your
attitude, your style, your choice of words,
everything you do and say.

If you feel warmth, radiate it!

If you feel exhilaration, jump with joy!

If you feel passion, exude it!

If you feel gratitude, show it!

If you feel anger, unleash it!

If you feel contentment, moo!

The whole idea is to express your feelings, but how can you do that if you don't allow them to show?

DEAR LITTLE SWEETHEART:
OF COURSE YOU WON'T KNOW
WHO I AM AT FIRST, BECAUSE YOU
HAVE SO MANY ADMIRERS; BUT WHEN I
TELL YOU THAT I'M THE ONE WITH THE
TWO EYES THAT CAN'T SEE ANYTHING BUT
YOU; THE TWO EARS THAT CAN'T HEAR
ANYTHING BUT YOUR VOICE; THE NOSE
THAT NEVER SMELT A FLOWER AS SWEET
AS YOUR BREATH; THE MOUTH THAT
TALKS OF NOTHING BUT YOUR
BEAUTY, AND THE TWO FEET
THAT WILL GO TO THE
WORLDS END TO PLEASE YOU,
YOU WILL KNOW AT
ONCE THAT IT'S ME!

> *Of all forms of caution,*
> *caution in love is perhaps the most*
> *fatal to true happiness.*
>
> BERTRAND RUSSELL

Here are some more ways to express what you feel:

1.
Always start by focusing on a particular feeling.

If it's vague, try to make it concrete. If there are two or more feelings involved, try to separate them. Try to put each feeling into words, not necessarily the words you want to end up with, just the words that will express the feeling and all of its nuances *to you.*

Writing them down will help tremendously because it's easier to develop a thought when you're looking at it on paper.

Never start out trying to think up clever words and phrases. The words will come when you've paved the way for them. The driving force that will make them come naturally is invariably the *feeling* that you want to convey.

So start with that feeling and stay with it. Apply all of your thought to it. Your object is to understand that feeling so well that the words will just naturally come.

Trust that they will.

2.
Choose colorful, vivid "picture" words, rather than colorless, abstract ones.

THESE ARE LESS INTERESTING AND DESCRIPTIVE	THAN THESE
pure white	snow white
perfectly clear	crystal clear
comfortable	cozy
walked	strolled
disarranged	wind-blown
very soft	creamy smooth
overfilled	overflowing
unstable	turbulent
climbing	soaring
touch	caress
very hot	red hot
burning	flaming
reflective	shimmering
angry	steaming
fell	tumbled
uneven	bumpy
cold	icy
stroke	pet

3.
Try to write sentences that are direct and active, rather than indirect and passive.

INDIRECT AND INACTIVE	DIRECT AND ACTIVE
Life was gloomy before you came along.	*You light up my life.*
There isn't anything I would really want to change about you.	*I like you just the way you are.*
There is no excuse for my behavior. Anyone who would act like that ought to beg forgiveness. Hope you'll forgive and forget. Love and kisses.	*I'm sorry! It was all my fault. Will you forgive me if I promise to never be like that again? And do you know how much I love you?*
Whatever we do to-gether is always great, whether it's walking or laughing, sitting and dreaming, or whatever.	*I like to walk with you. I like to laugh with you. I like to sit and dream with you. I like to do everything with you!*

4.
Use metaphors, analogies and similies.

Just don't let the terms scare you off. Understanding them and using them is simple.

These are phrases that describe something by borrowing interest from something else, that is usually unrelated to it in every way but one.

The Rock of Gibraltar, for example, has seemingly nothing to do with love, but because it is widely known as a symbol of strength and durability, it can be a fast and interesting way to communicate those qualities in love. As in *"My love for you is like the Rock of Gibraltar."*

Metaphors, analogies and similies all achieve the same purpose, the only telling difference is that similies start out with "like" or "as".

The purpose is to make a point stronger by putting it in the more dramatic terms of something else.

Here are some more examples:

You are the rainbow of my life.

I feel like the world's tallest mountain when I am with you.

The ship I'd been waiting for all my life arrived the day I met you.

You are the bluebird of my happiness.

You make my heart sing.

Your eyes are the mirrors of my soul.

However:

There are no techniques of verbal expression that are essential to the communication of your love.

Metaphors, analogies and similes can make your thoughts more interesting, when and if you decide to strive for them, and doing so is simple. But if you choose to ignore them forever, fine—your basic powers of expression are all you need.

The point I wanted to make is that vivid, colorful, active, emotionally charged words and phrases add interest to whatever you're trying to say. Which is why you see so many moons and stars and meadows and rainbows in the writings of romantic love.

Words are like the palette of colors available to a painter. They are your tools of expression. Within the simple guidelines of this book, use them as you choose.

5.
Whatever you say, make it straight from the heart.

Don't try to edit your feelings to conform with whatever your idea of "proper English" happens to be. Above all, never try to tone down the intensity or exuberance of your feelings because you think you might sound corny or juvenile.

Express your feelings just as you feel them, just as they come to you. Straight from the heart.

Not from the head, because the heart is always truer, more trustworthy. It also communicates to another heart better, because hearts speak an entirely different language than heads do.

Learn to listen to your heart. And above all, learn to trust it.

Try not to be influenced by the ways and words of others, so that only your purest feelings will travel from your heart to hers, or his.

*The heart has its reasons
which reason knows nothing of.*

PASCAL

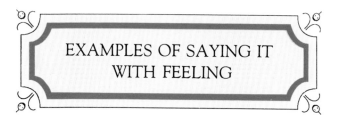

EXAMPLES OF SAYING IT WITH FEELING

Oh how strong the compulsion to shout to the heavens how much I love you! And to run and leap and sing and dance, just thinking of the incredible fact that you exist!

I can't get you out of my mind, or my heart, or my soul, and I hope and pray that I never do.

The luckiest day of my life was the day I found you.

Do you know that when I'm with you, I feel much taller than I normally do?

It's so wonderful to go to sleep at night and to know that, when I wake up in the morning, you'll be there beside me.

Just thinking about you can make me cry.

Being with you is like being in heaven!

The most wonderful feeling I've ever felt is the touch of your hand.

You are the coziest fireplace I've ever sat in front of.

You are the most beautiful sight that ever took my breath away!

Oh but I feel so sorry for you, because you'll never know the joy of loving you!

I wish you could be me for just one day, so you could know how much I love you.

Sometimes I feel that my heart will burst!

The first time I looked into your eyes was the first time I saw God.

No matter how far away you may be, I can always feel you.

You are God's masterpiece.

Being with you makes me soar like an eagle!

After all these years you still light up my days. And my nights!

9.

Make it you.

hat does the one you love really want from you? The answer is *you.* So that's what you ought to give. *You*, in your own style and your own words.

Don't try to write like a poet, unless that's what you really want to do. The point is, you don't have to write like a poet to say what you want to say, nor is that the standard you will be judged by.

What you will be judged by is feeling, thoughtfulness, enthusiasm and, most of all, sincerity. Could any poet convey those qualities to the one you love better than you?

Not Shakespeare himself.

Do everything your own way, and use anything that strikes your fancy. Words, sketches, paste-ons, anything that helps you say what you want to say.

If you feel an impulse to draw a funny face, draw one. And don't let the fact that you "can't draw" stop you. Anyone can draw stick figures. Or cut out a funny face from a newspaper or magazine and use it as is, or use it to draw or trace from.

Letting go of your inhibitions will add immeasurably to the enthusiasm that you feel and transmit. And in communication, enthusiasm is as contagious as it is credible.

Letting go of your inhibitions is also the best way to let out the real you.

The real you, and the assurance that you love him or her in your own way, in your own words. That's what he or she wants to hear and see from you. Nothing more, nothing less.

You are the one I love with all my heart. The one I most admire, respect and trust. The one who makes me happiest. I am yours and yours alone, forever. And don't you ever forget it!

Some more ways to help make it you.

Most people who have trouble expressing themselves in writing have one problem in common, and because it is seldom a problem of ability, it is seldom a difficult one to overcome.

In most cases, the problem, I am convinced, started with faulty teaching in the early grades, and grew worse as the lack of confidence became ingrained and opportunities to overcome it were increasingly evaded.

As a result, millions of otherwise competent, educated, often brilliant people tense up or freeze at the thought of having to write something original for the eyes of others. They lose all sense of looseness and become so rigid that a relaxed, easy, natural, conversational manner is impossible.

Could a baseball player *ever* get a hit if he always went up to bat like that?

Try to see and understand this problem for what it is, a matter of attitude. Which means it's within your control; you can do something about it.

The first thing you have to do is to change your attitude of no confidence and no hope to an optimistic one, which will come to you naturally as you put what you're learning into practice.

The next thing you have to do is a matter of technique, and it's probably the most important one there is.

Write like you talk.

Easily, naturally, confidently. Forget all the rules of grammar and syntax and sentence structure that are probably long forgotten anyway, and remember that all you're really trying to accomplish is to express your honest feelings in your own individual way.

Remember too, you are writing to only one person who is not going to judge you like an English teacher, because that person is your most understanding friend and is interested in just one thing: to know how you feel about her or him, in your own words.

How can you lose? Your audience is totally on your side, and all it wants is what you and you alone are capable of delivering. An honest expression of your love that will be as individual as your fingerprint.

So write it just as you would say it if he or she were there beside you.

I love you more than anything! Even my Corvette.

If it would be natural for you to say this to her, or to him, then it would be natural for you to write it. Either way, always try to express your most honest feelings, and the real you.

The obvious importance of being personal

It may seem out of place to even mention the importance of being personal within the context of love, because love is obviously the most personal thing there is. I am mentioning it only because so many people become so tense and rigid that anything they write tends to be stiff and impersonal.

It will help immeasurably to use personal words like "I" and "me" and "you" and "us" and "we" wherever they seem to apply.

Again, it should go without saying in love, but it may help to bear in mind that your object is to make your expressions as personally intimate, warm and caring as you possibly can.

Contractions help make it conversational.

Another way to help you write like you talk is to use contractions as liberally as you do in conversation. The two columns below will illustrate the difference:

The formal written way	The conversational way
Is not	Isn't
Would not	Wouldn't or won't
Do not	Don't
Would not	Wouldn't
Should not	Shouldn't
Would have	Would've
Should have	Should've
Cannot	Can't
I am	I'm
I will	I'll
We will	We'll
We were	We're
We have	We've
You are	You're
You will	You'll
You would	You'd
I would	I'd
I have	I've
There will	There'll
Are not	Aren't

It will also help to use unpretentious words and phrases rather than pretentious ones.

PRETENTIOUS	UNPRETENTIOUS
assistance	help
difficult	hard
pursue	chase
relate	tell
masculine	manly
deceased	dead
intoxicated	drunk
endeavor	try
curtailed	stopped
modify	change
preferable	better
observe	see
gratitude	thanks
inquire	ask
retain	keep
excellent	great
perspiration	sweat
employment	work
ascend	climb
enumerate	list
accelerate	speed up
apprehended	nabbed/caught
terminate	end
unpretentious	down to earth

Be charming but simple,
as if you
were talking to her.

OVID

10.

Above all, make it often.

Of all the things you have to do to express your love, this is the most important.

Remember that no human being ever lives a moment without feeling the need for love. It is perhaps the greatest of all human needs. We are born crying for it, and we die in greater need of it than ever before.

In romantic love it is the same, except that the need doesn't continue at the same constant rate. It continues at a constantly *increasing* rate.

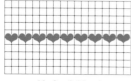

Need to feel loved throughout life in general.

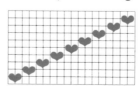

Need to feel loved throughout romantic life.

The reason is that the composition of romantic love is more complex and delicate than other forms of love. It involves the intricate needs of two joined yet separate and different human beings.

Each of them is in an almost constant state of need for the reassurance, reinforcement and renewal of the other's love.

Each of them may be sure of the other's love today, but tomorrow is another day, and each is a human being with all the doubts and insecurities of all human beings, especially those who live in the sensitive world of romantic love.

Always remember that the need for reassurance can never be satisfied "once and for all." So never assume that your loved one knows how much you love him or her and that, therefore, you don't have to keep saying it over and over.

You do.

And as long as you care, you always will.

Try to be sensitive to his or her doubts and insecurities; he or she has them just as you do.

The real soundness of a relationship can only be measured within the most private reaches of each person. Neither should ever assume that he or she knows what's going on inside the other, and that everything is just as it's always been.

A day can be a very long time in love, as can an hour or a minute.

Never, never, take love for granted!

Try to express your love as often as you did in the beginning, because that is the only way to keep it as alive and beautiful as it was in the beginning. Especially if you want it to grow deeper and ever more beautiful with the years.

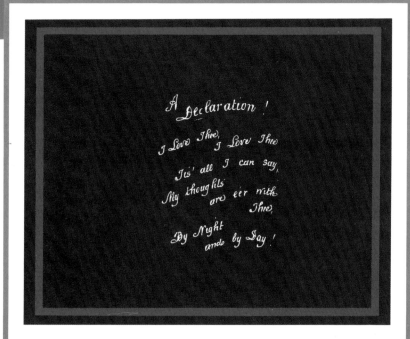

I want not only to be loved,
but to be told that I am loved.

GEORGE ELIOT

Here are some thought-starters for putting your love into words more often:

Shouldn't you say "I love you" or equivalent at least twice a day, as often as you brush your teeth? Don't say it just to meet your quota, but learn to *say it* whenever you *feel it*. Try to develop a connection between the feeling and the saying so that the saying just naturally follows the feeling.

Because you and your loved one are probably apart most of your waking hours, get into the habit of using the written word to supplement your spoken words. For example:

Put a note in his pocket before he leaves in the morning—a note, perhaps, expressing your interest in that big contract he's working on.

If you leave before she does in the morning, leave a note on the breakfast table expressing your thoughts and wishes for the day. And your love.

Tear items out of newspapers and magazines that you know will interest him, and add a note that expresses your interest. And your love.

Leave a note under her pillow the day you leave on a business trip.

 Put a note in his briefcase with no other purpose than to make a private joke, or just to say *"I'm thinking about you"* or *"I love you."* And sign it with a lipstick kiss.

 Pretend you're Robert or Elizabeth Browning and write a good old-fashioned love letter. Not necessarily as a substitute for the telephone, but as a more thoughtful, intimate and expressive way of communicating your deepeset feelings — in a form that can be read and re-read and treasured forever. For when it come to sheer romanticism, nothing can compare with a love letter. And you don't have to be miles away in order to write one. Try writing one on a special occasion, an anniversary for example, and compare its reception with that of the usual greeting card. As a gift, nothing can compare with it because no amount of money could buy it. Or how about a letter whose only purpose is to tell him, or her, how much you really care?

There is probably nothing you could ever do or say that would be more cherished than that. *I urge that you give the power and beauty of the love letter a try.*

> *More than kisses,*
> *letters mingle souls.*
>
> JOHN DONNE
>
>

You will of course come up with the best ideas yourself, because the more an idea is attuned to the realities of a relationship, the more effective it will be. All you have to do is let your imagination go.

It will require a bit of thought, time and effort, but the rewards will be more than worth it.

And then there's that obvious but often under-used idea known as the telephone. It's the most accessible way to express your love when you and your loved one are apart. It costs to use it, of course, but think of it as an investment — in the best love insurance you could possibly buy.

*The supreme happiness of life
is the conviction
that we are loved.*

VICTOR HUGO

And now,
with this important clarification,
we have come to the end.

Most of what you have just learned has concerned the written word as opposed to the spoken word, only because the written word represents a deeper blockage for a greater number of people. Not because the written word is more important, because in the expression of love, it is actually the other way around.

Of all the ways there are to express your love, the most direct and convincing is to simply say *"I love you"*—as honestly as you feel it. The only problem is that, in spite of the best intentions, it gets said less and less as the days and years go by.

So as the demands upon our time and attention increase, and because we can't always be there to express our feelings face to face, most of us come to rely more and more on the Valentines and the birthday cards to say it for us.

And there is nothing wrong with that, as long as we use such purchased sentiments as reinforcements to, and not replacements for, our own face-to-face communication.

But too many people, probably the overwhelming majority, rely on them almost entirely, and add little more of themselves than the signing of their name. Of course, you know by now how wrong that is, because to repeat what has been said throughout this book, no one can express your love as effectively as you can.

We ought to say *"I love you"* or its equivalent as often as we have the feeling, and if we don't have the feeling very often, then something else is wrong.

Yet as vitally important as the spoken word is, it is not the most important element in the expression of our love.

The most important element is our actions. An affectionate hug, a tender kiss, an empathetic wink or an unexpected display of exceptional thoughtfulness expresses our feelings, our real feelings, far more effectively than all of the words in the dictionary ever could.

So always remember this order of importance:

1. Actions.
2. Spoken words.
3. Written words.

*They do not love
that do not show their love.*

JOHN HEYWOOD

Valediction

You are now prepared to start freeing yourself of your inhibitions, to start putting your love into words, to start putting into practice what you have learned.

And what you have learned is everything you need to start saying what you want to say, in words that you will soon be proud of. There is nothing that you need to do now that is beyond you, nothing that demands any special gifts other than the one of love that you already have.

So start putting what you now know into practice, not some day when the mood strikes you but today and tomorrow and the next day, and you'll soon be expressing your feelings with ease and confidence.

And perhaps one day you'll write and tell me how this book helped you, or how it didn't, or how it might have helped you better.

I would be thrilled to share the joy of any success I may have helped you achieve, and to see how good you've become at expressing your thoughts and feelings.

Now go out into the world and express your love. Straight from the heart!

Appendix

How the poets
put their love into words

How do I love thee? Let me count the ways. I love thee to the depth and breadth my soul can reach...I love thee with the breath, smiles, tears, of all my life! And, if God choose, I shall but love thee better after death.

—ROBERT BROWNING

And I, who looked only for God, found thee.

—ELIZABETH BARRETT BROWNING

My heart is like a singing bird.

—CHRISTINA ROSSETTI

Things that are lovely can tear my heart in two, moonlight on still pools, You.

—DOROTHY DOW

I shall love you in December with the love I gave in May!

—JOHN ALEXANDER JOYCE

This bud of love, by summer's ripening breath, May prove a beauteous flower when next we meet.

—WILLIAM SHAKESPEARE

Love that endures, from Life that disappears.

—ROBERT BROWNING

For verily love knows not "mine" or "thine;" With separate "I" and "thou" free love has done, For one is both and both are one in love.

—CHRISTINA ROSSETTI

For one man in my world of all the men This wide world holds; O love, my world is you.

—CHRISTINA ROSSETTI

Behold me! I am worthy of thy loving,
For I love thee.
                    —ELIZABETH BARRETT BROWNING

I cannot love thee as I ought,
For love reflects the thing beloved.
                    —ALFRED TENNYSON

Oh love! Oh love! whose shafts of fire
Invade the soul with sweet surprise.
                    —EURIPIDES

Sure he that loves his lady 'cause she's fair,
Delights his eye, so loves himself, not her.
Something there is moves me to love, and I
Do know I love, but know not how, nor why.
                    —ALEXANDER BROME

Like these cool lilies may our loves remain,
Perfect and pure, and know not any stain.
                    —ANDREW LANG

Yet love consumes me, for what bounds are there to
love?
                    —VIRGIL

My clouds arise all flushed with glory;
I love, and the world is mine!
                    —FLORENCE EARLE COATES

With love that scorns the lapse of time,
And ties that stretch beyond the deep.
                    —THOMAS CAMPBELL

Give me purity to be worthy the good in her, and
grant her patience to reach the good in me.
                    —GEORGE MEREDITH

Thou wast all that to me, love,
For which my soul did pine:
A green isle in the sea, love,
A fountain and a shrine.
—EDGAR ALLAN POE

Quick as a humming bird is my love,
Dipping into the hearts of flowers,
She darts so eagerly, swiftly, sweetly
Dipping into the flowers of my heart.
—JAMES OPPENHEIM

Good night, good night! Parting is such sweet sorrow
That I shall say good night till it be morrow.
—WILLIAM SHAKESPEARE

Give me a kiss, and to that kiss a score.
Then to that twenty, add a hundred more.
A thousand to that hundred, so kiss on,
To make that thousand up a million.
Treble that million, and when that is done,
Let's kiss afresh, as when we first begun.
—ROBERT HERRICK

Oh that the desert were my dwelling place,
With one fair spirit for my minister,
That I might all forget the human race,
And, hating no one, love but only her!
—LORD BYRON

To stray together down Life's slope,
While Age came on like gentle rain.
—R.U. JOHNSON

I love thee like pudding; if thou were pie I'd eat thee.

—JOHN RAY

With all thy faults, I love thee still.

— WILLIAM COWPER

What are the fields, or flow'rs, or all I see?
Ah, tasteless all, if not enjoy'd with thee.

—THOMAS PARNELL

And neither the angels in heaven above,
Nor the demons down under the sea,
Can ever dissever my soul from the soul
Of the beautiful Annabel Lee.

—EDGAR ALLAN POE

He kissed the ground her feet did kiss.

—JOHN DAVIDSON

I love thee, love thee!
'Tis all that I can say;
It is my vision in the night,
My dreaming in the day.

—THOMAS HOOD

And in his heart my heart is locked,
And in his life my life.

—CHRISTINA ROSSETTI

Banish that fear; my flame can never waste,
For love sincere refines upon the taste.

—COLLEY CIBBER

Escape me? Never, beloved! While I am I, and you are you.

—ROBERT BROWNING

O tell her, brief is life but love is long.
—ALFRED TENNYSON

Say thou dost love me, love me, love me — toll
The silver iterance! — only minding, Dear,
To love me also in silence, with thy soul.
—ELIZABETH BARRETT BROWNING

I love thee, as the good love heaven.
—HENRY WADSWORTH LONGFELLOW

Now passion's waves of conflict o'er her rush:
The sob, the tear, the pallid brow reveal
How wildly strong the love her heart and spirit feel.
—CHARLOTTE BRONTE

Heaven would not be Heaven were thy soul not
with mine,
Nor would Hell be Hell were our two souls together.
—BAPISTA MANTUANUS

She floats upon the river of his thoughts!
—HENRY WADSWORTH LONGFELLOW

Let thy love in kisses rain...
—PERCY SHELLEY

Thou art my love, my life, my heart,
The very eyes of me:
And hast command of every part
To live and die for thee.
—ROBERT HERRICK

She whom I love is hard to catch and conquer,
Hard, but O the glory of the winning were she
won!
—GEORGE MEREDITH

So dear I love him, that with him all deaths I could
endure, without him live no life.

—JOHN MILTON

You'll love me yet! — and I can tarry
Your love's protracted growing.
June reared that bunch of flowers you carry,
From seeds of April's sowing.

—ROBERT BROWNING

If love were what the rose is,
And I were like the leaf,
Our lives would grow together
In sad or singing weather.

—ALGERNON SWINBURNE

Nothing in the world is single;
All things, by a law divine,
In one another's being mingle,
Why not I with thine?

—PERCY SHELLEY

My bounty is as boundless as the sea,
My love as deep; the more I give to thee
The more I have, for both are infinite.

—WILLIAM SHAKESPEARE

Art thou not dearer to my eyes than light?
Dost thou not circulate through all my veins?
Mingle with life, and form my very soul?

—EDWARD YOUNG

Lukewarmness I account a sin,
As great in love as in religion.

—ABRAHAM COWLEY

The seamen on the wave, love,
When storm and tempest rave, love,
Look to one star to save, love,
Thou art that star to me!

—JOHN TYLER

We have lived and loved together
Through many changing years;
We have shared each other's gladness,
And wept each other's tears.

—CHARLES JEFFERYS

Beloved, let us love so well,
Our work shall still be better for our love,
And still our love be sweeter for our work.

—ELIZABETH BARRETT BROWNING

A hundred years should go to praise
Thine eyes and on thy forehead gaze;
Two hundred to adore each breast,
But thirty thousand to the rest;
An age at least to every part,
And the last age should show your heart.

—ANDREW MARVELL

Tho' near the gates of Paradise,
Gladly I'd turn away,
Just to hear you say, "I love you!"
Sometime, somewhere, some day.

—RIDA JOHNSON YOUNG

Our state cannot be severed; we are one,
One flesh; to lose thee would be to lose myself.

—JOHN MILTON

Think of my loyal love, my last adieu;
Absence and love are naught if we are true.
—ALFRED DE MUSSET

If thou must love me, let it be for nought
Except for love's sake only.
—ELIZABETH BARRETT BROWNING

Love is kindest, and hath most length,
The kisses are most sweet,
When it's enjoyed in heat of strength,
Where like affections meet.
—PATRICK HANNAY

To meet you grows almost a pang,
Because the pang of parting comes so soon.
—CHRISTINA ROSSETTI

Sing the Lover's Litany;
"Love like ours can never die."
—RUDYARD KIPLING

Love is indestructible.
Its holy flame burneth,
From Heaven it came,
To Heaven returneth.

O. B ?

1983.

100

timeless thoughts on love

At the very least,
you'll find these
highly credentialed
quotations interesting
to read and to reflect
upon. You should
also find them
helpful in your own
communication of
love, as inspiration to
your thoughts or as a
persuasive way to
make a point.

I want not only to be loved, but to be told that I am loved.

—GEORGE ELIOT

Love is that condition in which the happiness of another person is essential to your own joy.

—ROBERT A. HEINLEIN

Love consists in desiring to give what is our own to another and feeling his delight as our own.

—SWEDENBORG

Love is to feel with one's whole self the existence of another.

—UNKNOWN

Tell me how much one loves and I will tell you how much he has seen of God.

—UNKNOWN

Love is patient. Love is kind. Love is not jealous, it does not put on airs, it is not snobbish. Love is never rude, it is not self-seeking, it is not prone to anger; neither does it brood over injuries. Love does not rejoice in what is wrong, but rejoices in the truth. There is no limit to love's forebearance, its truth, its hope, its power to endure.

—ST. PAUL TO THE CORINTHIANS

There is only one kind of love, but there are a thousand imitations.

—LA ROCHEFOUCAULD

True love is like ghosts, which everybody talks about and few have seen.

—LA ROCHEFOUCAULD

*The joining of spirits, even momentarily, is rare.
The joining of bodies is so much easier and so much
less intimate.*

—TENNESSEE WILLIAMS

*I have never known love. But if it is like two
invisible lines stretching from my spirit to your
spirit, then I am in love.*

—HELEN KELLER

*In their choice of lovers, both male and female
reveal their true nature. The type of human being
we prefer reveals the contours of our heart.*

— ORTEGA Y GASSET

*Love is of all the passions the strongest, for it
attacks simultaneously the head, the heart and
the senses.*

—VOLTAIRE

*There is nothing holier, in this life of ours, than the
first consciousness of love, the first fluttering of its
silken wings.*

—HENRY WADSWORTH LONGFELLOW

*The man who is in love for the first time, even if
his love is unrequitted, is a Godlike being.*

— HEINRICH HEINE

*Never forget that the most powerful force on earth
is love.*

— NELSON ROCKEFELLER

Where love is, there is no lack.

—RICHARD BROME

That love is all there is, is all we know of love.

—EMILY DICKENSON

Love looks not with the eyes, but the mind; and therefore is winged Cupid painted blind.
—WILLIAM SHAKESPEARE

All of life is an attempt to escape loneliness—the search for another warm body. (Charlotte Chandler: 'And a warm mind'?) That's the ultimate sex, if it can ever be achieved. That's when the nightingale sings.
—TENNESSEE WILLIAMS

What is love without passion? A garden without flowers, a hat without feathers, tobogganing without snow.
—JENNIE JEROME CHURCHILL

It is easier to kill, than to tame, a lover's passion.
—OVID

Plenty destroys passion.
—OVID

Love's tongue is in the eyes.
—PHINEAS FLETCHER

A lover's eyes will gaze an eagle blind.
—WILLIAM SHAKESPEARE

Love, and a cough, cannot be hid.
—GEORGE HERBERT

In the one we love, we find our second self. Love is the beauty of the soul. To love abundantly is to live abundantly, to love forever is to live forever. There is exquisite beauty in the heart that cares and loves. Love believes all things, hopes all things, endures all things.
—UNKNOWN

Love is liking someone better than you like yourself.
— FRANK TYGER

Great thoughts come from the heart.
— DE VAUVENARGUES

The heart has its reasons which reason knows nothing of.
— BLAISE PASCAL

We are all born for love. It is the principle of existence and its only end.
— DISRAELI-SYBIL

Love in its essence is spiritual fire.
— SWEDENBORG

Adam could not be happy even in paradise without Eve.
— JOHN LUBBOCK

Love is like a rose, the joy of all the earth.
— CHRISTINA ROSSETTI

Love comforteth like sunshine after rain.
— WILLIAM SHAKESPEARE

Love is a sunshine mixed with rain.
— SIR WALTER RALEIGH

The music that reaches farthest into heaven is the beating of a loving heart.
— HENRY WARD BEECHER

What's the earth with all its art, verse, music worth— compared with love, found, gained, and kept?
— ROBERT BROWNING

One word frees us from all the weight and pain of life; that word is love.

—SOPHOCLES

Love is the triumph of imagination over intelligence.

—H.L. MENCKEN

Love is the poetry of the senses.

—HONORE DE BALZAC

In jealousy, there is more self-love than love.

—LA ROCHEFOUCAULD

If love does not know how to give and take without restrictions, it is not love.

—EMMA GOLDMAN

Love must be given without thought of reciprocation.

—FRANK TYGER

Love is not getting, but giving.

—HENRY VAN DYKE

The only present love demands is love.

—JOHN GAY

You can give without loving, but you can never love without giving.

—UNKNOWN

More than kisses, letters mingle souls.

—JOHN DONNE

The heart is a brittle thing, and one false vow can break it.

—E.G. BULVER-LYTTON

We pardon to the extent that we love.

—LA ROCHEFOUCAULD

Love is swift, sincere, pious, pleasant, gentle, strong, patient, faithful, prudent, long-suffering, manly and never seeking her own; for wheresoever a man seeketh his own, there he falleth from love.
—THOMAS A. KEMPIS

Love has no thought of self! Love sacrifices all things to bless the thing it loves.
—BULWER LYTTON

All for love, nothing for reward.
—EDMUND SPENSER

Love is love's reward.
—JOHN DRYDEN

To love is to believe, to hope, to know; 'tis an essay, a taste of heaven below.
—EDMUND WALLER

Love sought is good, but given unsought is better.
—WILLIAM SHAKESPEARE

Love conquers all.
—VIRGIL

Whoso loves believes the impossible.
—ELIZABETH BARRETT BROWNING

All love is sweet, given or returned. They who inspire it most are fortunate, but those who feel it most are happier still.
—PERCY SHELLEY

The pleasure of love is in loving. We are happier in the passion we feel than in that we arouse.
—LA ROCHEFOUCAULD

Love cannot be bought or stolen. It can only be given away.

—FORTUNE COOKIE

Love between man and woman is really just a kind of breathing.

—D.H. LAWRENCE

True affection is a body of enigmas, mysteries and riddles, wherein two so become one that they both become two.

—THOMAS BROWNE

What is a kiss? The sure, sweet cement, glue and lime of love.

—ROBERT HERRICK

If two stand shoulder to shoulder against the gods, happy together, the gods themselves are helpless against them, while they stand so.

—MAXWELL ANDERSON

Love never reasons but profusely gives, gives like a thoughtless prodigal its all, and trembles then lest it has done too little.

—UNKNOWN

To be able to say how much you love is to love but little.

—PETRARCH

I cannot love thee as I ought, for love reflects the thing beloved.

—ALFRED TENNYSON

Yet love consumes me; for what bounds are there to love?

—VIRGIL

It is the special quality of love not to be able to remain stationary, to be obliged to increase under pain of diminishing.

—ANDRE GIDE

In love and war, don't give counsel.

— FRENCH PROVERB

Love lieth deep; love dwells not in lip-depths.

—ALFRED TENNYSON

To be loved is the dearest wish of the heart.

—UNKNOWN

The supreme happiness of life is the conviction that we are loved.

—VICTOR HUGO

There is no heaven like mutual love.

—GEORGE GRANVILLE

Love is a butterfly which, when pursued is just beyond your grasp, but if you will sit down quietly, it may alight upon you.

—NATHANIEL HAWTHORNE

Only a wise man knows how to love.

—SENECA

He is not a lover who does not love for ever.

—EURIPIDES

O tell her, brief is life but love is long.

—ALFRED TENNYSON

Unless you can swear "For life, for death!"— oh, fear to call it loving!

—ELIZABETH BARRETT BROWNING

You will find, as you look back upon your life, that the moments that stand out, the moments when you have really lived, are the moments when you have done things in the spirit of love.

—HENRY DRUMMOND

We are shaped and fashioned by what we love.

—GOETHE

We learn only from those we love.

—GOETHE

The great acts of love are done by those who habitually perform small acts of kindness.

—UNKNOWN

They do not love that do not show their love.

—JOHN HEYWOOD

Love is never lost. If not reciprocated, it will flow back to soften and purify the heart.

—WASHINGTON IRVING

It is sad not to be loved, but it is much sadder not to be able to love.

—MIGUEL DE UNAMUNO

'Tis better to have loved and lost than never to have loved at all.

—ALFRED TENNYSON

For winning love, we run the risk of losing.

—THOMAS HARDY

They that love beyond the world cannot be separated by it. Death cannot kill what never dies; they live in one another still.

—WILLIAM PENN

Of all forms of caution, caution in love is perhaps most fatal to true happiness.

—BERTRAND RUSSELL

People who are sensible about love are incapable of it.

— DOUGLAS YATES

As love is the cause of the greatest ills that men suffer, it is the cause also of the most perfect pleasures, consisting only in extremities; and as many as are made miserable by love, none are made happy without love.

—ALGERNON SIDNEY

There is no remedy for love but to love more.

—HENRY THOREAU

Let no one who loves be called unhappy. Even love unreturned has its rainbow.

—JAMES MATTHEW BARRIE

It is best to love wisely, no doubt, but to love foolishly is better than not to love at all.

—WILLIAM THACKERAY

To love and win is the best thing; to love and lose the next best.

—WILLIAM THACKERAY

Pains of love be sweeter far, than all other pleasures are.

—JOHN DRYDEN

Oh, there's nothing in life like making love!

—THOMAS HOOD

To love and be loved is the greatest joy on earth.

—UNKNOWN

Love
expressed
is love
enhanced.

J AMES D. D ONOVAN

 JAMES D. DONOVAN has been a highly creative communicator for many years. As vice president of Carson/Roberts, Los Angeles, the West's most creative advertising agency, and of its successor, the world-renowned Ogilvy & Mather, he produced a wealth of pattern-breaking advertising for companies like Learjet, Flying Tigers, Technicolor and Lincoln-Mercury.

Since 1973 he has been working in his own name, as James D. Donovan, Inc. His award winning annual reports for Dataproducts have been widely acclaimed for their honesty and imagination, and his spirited advertising for Burlington Northern Air Freight sparked its surge from upstart among 350 companies to No. 2 in six years.

His working purpose is expressed in his philosophic trademark: *Excellence is everything. Because mediocrity is nothing.*

But perhaps the most interesting part of his background, in relation to this book, began in 1981 when he became a communicator for himself, in the much chancier field of romantic love.

How to communicate the intensity of his feelings, and to understand the miracle that was taking place within him? A large part of the answer, not surprisingly, took the form of written and visual expression, the tools of his trade.

"I kept saying I couldn't find the words," he

recalls, "and I knew I never would. Yet I was compulsively driven to try, and out of my attempts came the most inspired words I'd ever written. My entire world became so inspired that, overnight, it motivated a whole new spiritual and physical me. I felt like an eagle that had just learned how to fly."

That was on his end. On the other end, the response was not on the same plane, although he would persist for five years before conceding that romantic love is an exception to the words he had put up on his wall, "Nothing is impossible to a willing heart."

So with a world of unfulfilled feelings pent up within and, coincidentally, a desire to start communicating to a broader audience than the corporate world, he chose the expression of love as the subject for his first book.

Many of the thoughts and feelings that he first expressed on his own behalf appear in this book. If they work as intended for the many who will now be exposed to them, he feels that his unsuccessful efforts may yet end up successful. On a far wider and, he says with a wince, perhaps even more gratifying scale than if they had achieved their original purpose.

May it turn out just that way. A happy ending for one and all. *Love expressed, love enhanced.*

Early 1800s Valentine from the Hallmark Historical Collection